Let's Read and Write
... that's it!

W0222646

Workbook 3

Susanne McCafferty
Tina Kresse

illustriert von
Elisabeth Lottermoser

Bestell-Nr. 1902-34 · ISBN 978-3-619-19234-2

Internetadresse: www.mildenberger-verlag.de
E-Mail: info@mildenberger-verlag.de

Auflage 4 3 2 1
Jahr 2013 2012 2011 2010

Druck: Kehler Druck GmbH & Co. KG, 77694 Kehl

Gedruckt auf umweltfreundlichen Papieren

Mildenberger Verlag

Inhalt

Hello Again – About Me

What's your name?

____

How old are you?

____

Where do you live?

____

Where do you come from?

____

What are your hobbies?

____

____

Who are your friends?

____

Which languages do you speak?

____

Hello Again – Portfolio: Me

This is what I look like.

Draw a picture or glue in a photo of yourself.

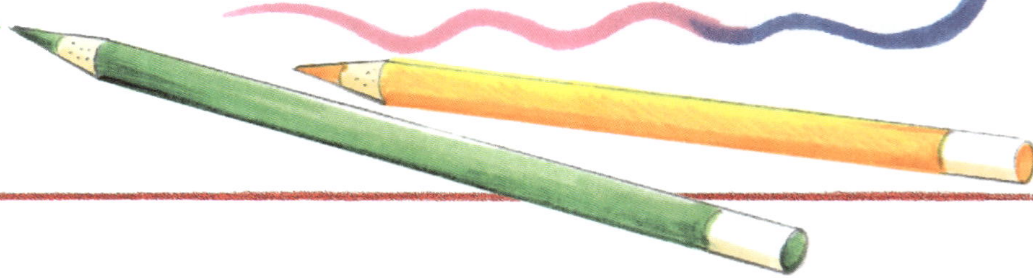

Hello Again – What´s Your Name?

These are the children in the workbook:

Anna and Michael are brother and sister and come from Edinburgh in Scotland.
Anna is nine years old, Michael is ten.
Anna is wearing a red, green, white and yellow T-shirt.
Michael is wearing an orange T-shirt.
Anna: “My hobbies are swimming and playing volleyball.”
Michael: “My hobbies are playing handball and riding my bike.”

What’s his name?

His name is ______________________ .

How old is he?

He is ________ years old.

Where does he come from?

He comes from

________________________________ .

Where does he live?

He lives in ________________________ .

What are his hobbies?

His hobbies are ____________________

____

____

What’s her name?

Her name is ______________________ .

How old is she?

She is ________ years old.

Where does she come from?

She comes from

____________________________ , too.

Where does she live?

She lives in ___________________ , too.

What are her hobbies?

Her hobbies are ____________________

____

____

Numbers and Colours – Let´s Count to 20

1. Write the number words under the sacks.

1	2	3	4	5
______	______	______	______	______
6	7	8	9	10
______	______	______	______	______
11	12	13	14	15
______	______	______	______	______
16	17	18	19	20
______	______	______	______	______

sixteen seven one eleven seventeen five
fourteen two nine nineteen twenty eight three
twelve fifteen thirteen six ten four eighteen

Numbers and Colours – Number Salad

1. Can you find the numbers? Connect the numbers to the words.

2. Find your own numbers! Connect the numbers and write the words.
   Colour a space in the left wheel and a space in the right wheel in the same colour.
   Write the number.

thirty	+	six	=	thirty-six
	+		=	
	+		=	
	+		=	
	+		=	
	+		=	
	+		=	
	+		=	
	+		=	

Numbers and Colours

1. Please colour the T-shirts and jeans in the right colours.

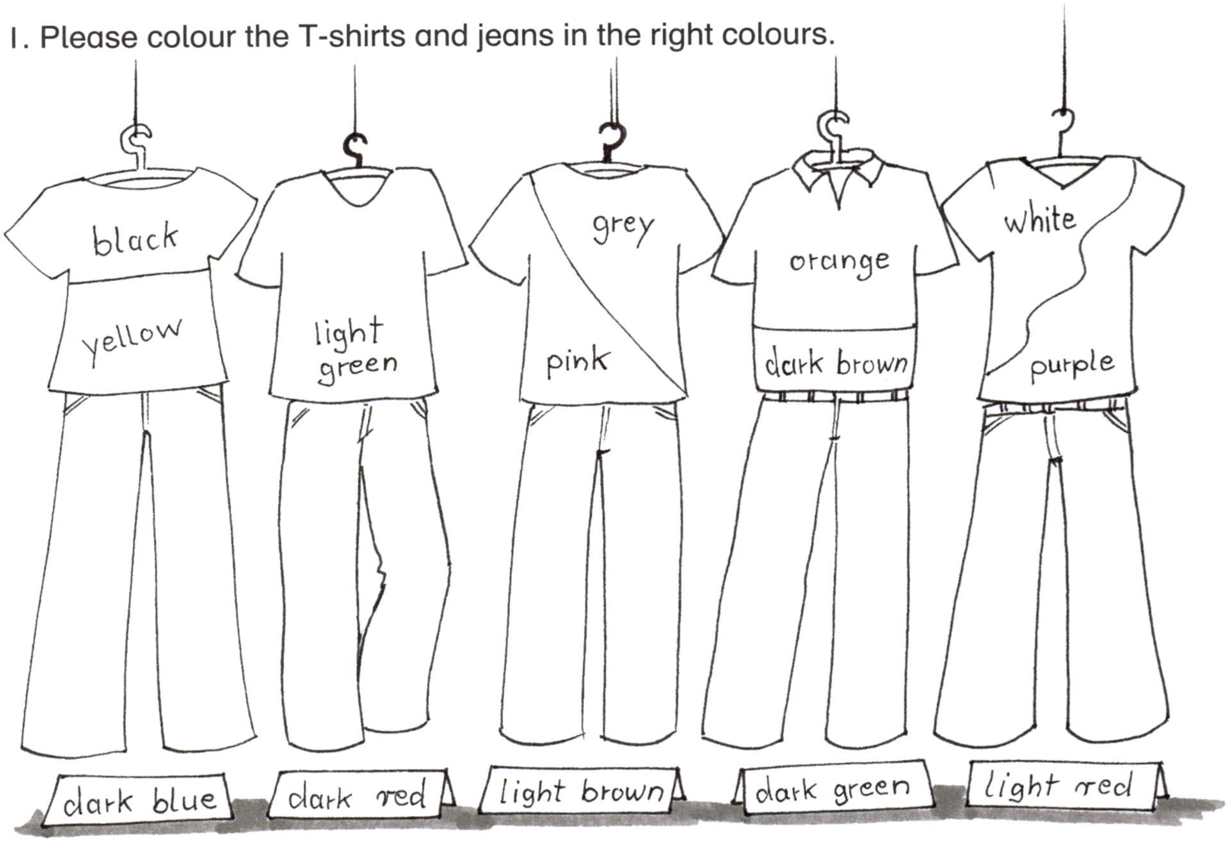

2. Colour these jeans and T-shirts as you like and write the colours in the boxes.

Numbers and Colours – Anna Buys Clothes

1. Underline the colour words in the text.

Anna Buys Clothes

Anna always wears blue jeans and a red, green, white and yellow T-shirt. Her mum does not like that. Today Anna and her mum go shopping. Anna says: “I’d like blue jeans and a red, green, white and yellow T-shirt.” “Anna!” her mum shouts. The shop assistant brings many T-shirts and many pairs of jeans. “Look, here is a light red T-shirt and a black pair of jeans.” Anna does not like red. “Look, here is a pink T-shirt and a purple pair of jeans.” the shop assistant says. But Anna doesn’t like pink and she doesn’t like purple. “Look, here is a light green T-shirt and a grey pair of jeans,” her mum says. She says: “But I want blue jeans and a red, green, white and yellow T-shirt.” The shop assistant has an idea. “Look Anna, I’ve got a white dress with red, green and yellow flowers. Do you like it?” Anna is happy. “Yes, that’s great,” she says. She is very happy.

2. Can you read the text?

3. Fill in the missing words.

In the shop there are many jeans and T-shirts.
There is

a ________________ T-shirt and a ________________ pair of jeans,

a ________________ T-shirt and a ________________ pair of jeans,

a ________________ T-shirt and a ________________ pair of jeans.

But Anna does not like them.

So she buys a ________________ dress with ________________ ,

________________ and ________________ flowers.

Anna is ________________________ .

Numbers and Colours

1. Colour in the T-shirts as you like.

2. What colour are your T-shirts?

Number ______________________ is ______________________

Number ______________________ is ______________________

Number ______________________ is ______________________

Number ______________________ is ______________________

Number ______________________ is ______________________

Number ______________________ is ______________________

Number ______________________ is ______________________

Number ______________________ is ______________________

Number ______________________ is ______________________

Number ______________________ is ______________________

____

____

Portfolio: Hello Again – Numbers and Colours

I can introduce myself.

My name is ______________________ . I'm ________ years old.

I live in ______________________________________

My hobbies are ____

____

I come from __________________________________

I know big numbers and many colours.
I can write the names of five numbers over 30:

____

____

I can write 7 different colours:

____

Diese Zahlen, Farben und Sätze kann ich noch auf Englisch schreiben:

____

____

____

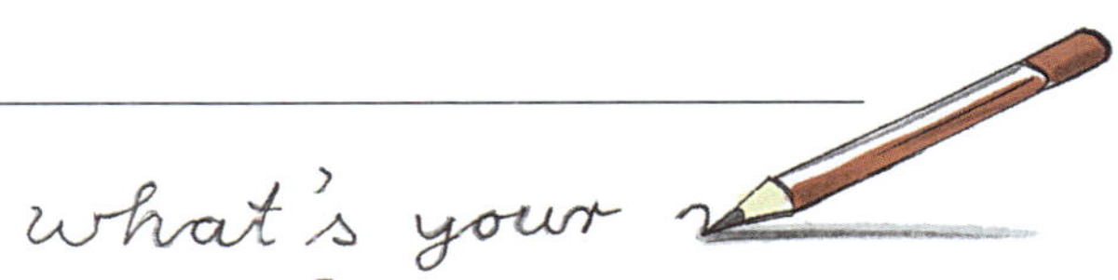

That was 

Portfolio: Hello Again – Numbers and Colours

Ich kann schon auf Englisch verstehen:

- wenn sich mir jemand vorstellt
- wenn mir jemand sagt, wie alt er ist und wo er wohnt
- wenn mir jemand sagt, wo er herkommt und was seine Hobbies sind
- die Zahlen, die mir jemand sagt
- die Farben, die mir jemand sagt
- in welchen Farben ich etwas anmalen soll

Ich kann schon auf Englisch sagen:

- wie ich heiße
- wie alt ich bin und wo ich wohne
- wo ich herkomme und was meine Hobbies sind
- wie eine Zahl heißt
- wie eine Farbe heißt
- welche Farben die Gegenstände haben

Ich kann schon auf Englisch fragen:

- wie jemand heißt
- wie alt jemand ist und wo jemand wohnt
- wo jemand herkommt und was seine Hobbies sind
- welche Farbe etwas hat
- wie viele Gegenstände da sind

Ich kann schon auf Englisch lesen:

- die Zahlwörter
- die Farben
- wenn sich jemand vorstellt
- welche Farbe etwas hat
- wie viele Gegenstände da sind

Ich bin mit mir sehr zufrieden.

Ich finde, es war schon ganz gut.

Ich hoffe, das wird noch besser.

At School – In My Schoolbag

1. In your schoolbag there are many things.
   Please write down what you can find in your schoolbag.

In my schoolbag there is ____

____

____

2. In your classroom there are many things, too.
   Please write down what you can find in your classroom.

In my classroom there is ____

____

____

At School – … that´s it!-Song

1. This is Anna's and Michael's classroom.
   Please draw or colour in the missing things.

There is a sponge in the wash-basin.

There are five books in the bookshelf.

There are ten exercise-books on the little cupboard.

The teacher's desk is green.

On two tables there are pencil-cases.

Next to three tables there are schoolbags.

2. In our song text there are some words missing.
   Can you fill them in?

When we go to school, what do we need?

Exercise-book, _ _ _ _ _ _ , glue.

When we go to school, what do we need?

_ _ _ _ _ _ _ _ _ , pen and ruler, too.

Chorus:

_ _ _ _ _ _ _ is easy, English is easy, oh – that's it!

English is easy, English is _ _ _ _ , oh – that's it! That's it!

At School – Rules in the Classroom

1. All children want a good atmosphere in the classroom.
   So the teacher tells them some rules:

2. Fill in the missing words.

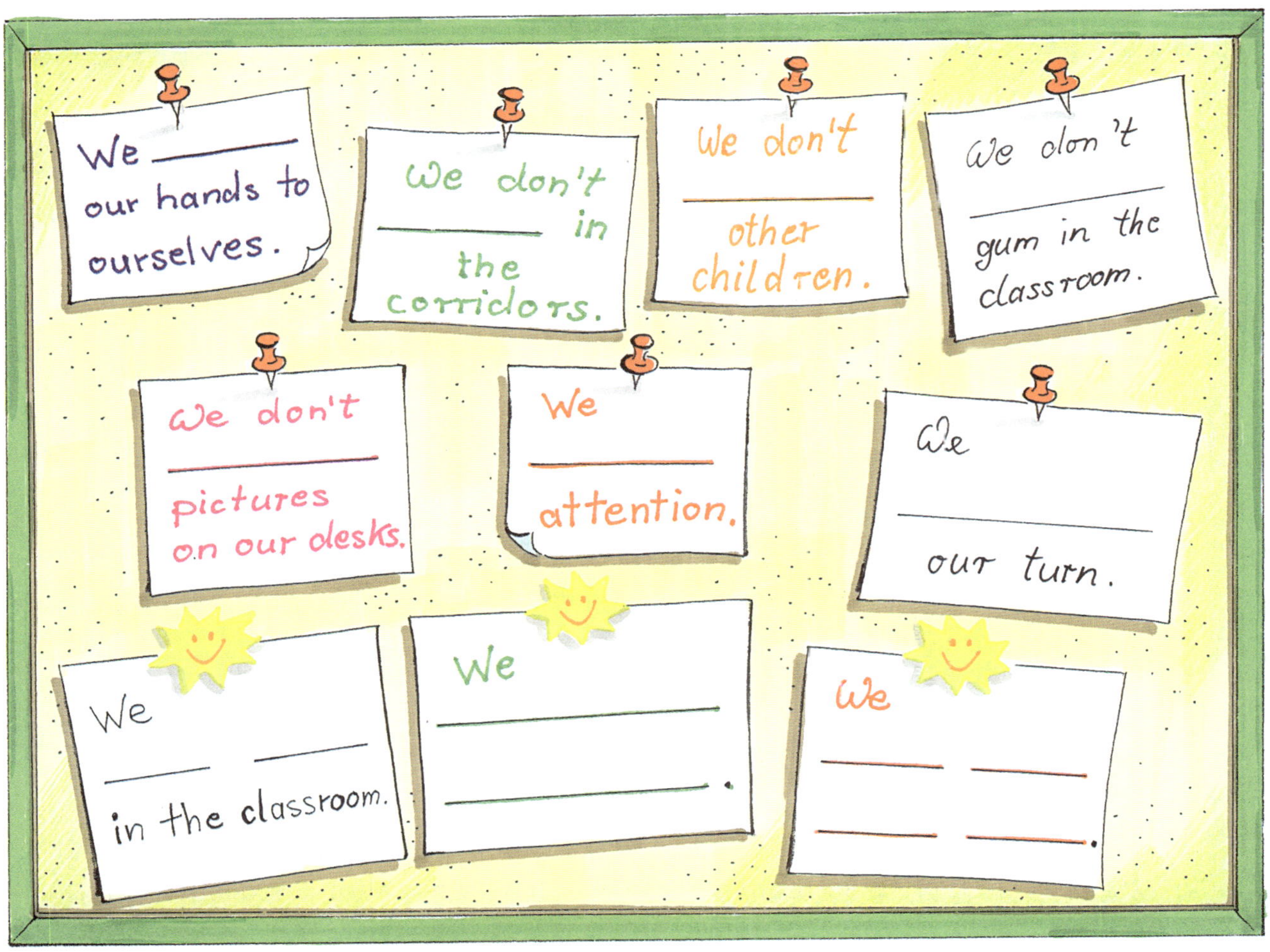

Halloween

1. Fill in the right words and draw arrows.

witch

~~witch~~ vampire pumpkin cauldron ghost rat bat broom spider frog hat

2. What is it?

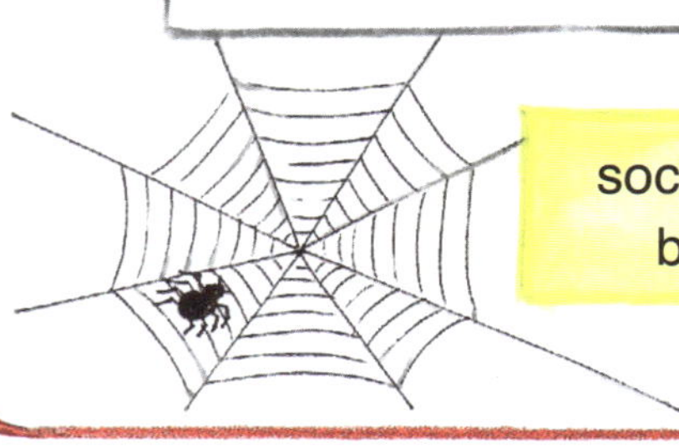

sock chocolate ghost biscuits vampire witch bat
black cat pumpkin jelly frogs hat red lemonade

Halloween

1. Can you read the text? The pictures will help you.

The Witch With the Hat

At Halloween Anna dressed up as a with a .

Michael was dressed up as a .

They took an old and created a little .

A man said: "A with a and a with a !"

They got . A went with them.

A woman said: "A with a and a and a with a !"

They got . A little boy dressed up as a went with them.

A young woman said: "A with a and a
and a with a and a !"

They got many green .

An old lady said: "A with a and a
and a with a and a and many !"

They got to drink. They went home. In front of the house there was a .

Anna's and Michael's parents said: "Oh here they are:
Our with a and a and the with a
and a and many . But you must go to bed now."

The little went home. Anna and Michael went to bed.

Anna dreamt of a with a and a
and a with a and a and many and a .

Halloween

1. Fill in the missing words.

Vampire Rock (Rock around the clock)

It's midnight time at twelve o'clock,

the ghosts get ready for the _ _ _ _ _ _ _ rock.

The _ _ _ _ _ _ is boiling and the _ _ _ _ _ _ _

is grinning, toads and _ _ _ _ _ and mice are singing,

_ _ _ _ _ _ and wizard, _ _ _ and _ _ _,

and all the ghosts have fun and chat.

Time is over, it's one o'clock,

the _ _ _ _ _ _ must finish their vampire rock.

Chorus:

And the teeth are rattling and the bones are shaking,

they are dancing till the dawn is breaking.

At night at night at night in the full moonlight.

witch
frogs
vampire
bat
cat
ghosts
potion
pumpkin

2. Here are many words. Which words do you need at Halloween? Colour them in red (blood red!)

ghost apple school rubber rat exercise-book vampire

witch ruler pencil black cat frog budgie toad draw

jeans pumpkin book grinning sit bat dog trick write

class mouse hat T-shirt pen black treat hamster

pizza book night blue water banana dress up schoolbag

Which letter do you get?

◯ **B** like bat, ◯ **V** like vampire or ◯ **W** like witch?

Portfolio: At School

I know what's in my schoolbag.

In my schoolbag there is ____

____.

I can name the things in my classroom.

In my classroom there is ____

____.

I can tell what we do at school.

We ____________________ in our exercise-books. We ________________ books.

We ________________ pictures. We ________________ to other children.

We ____________________________ . We ____________________________ .

Diese Wörter und Sätze über die Schule kann ich noch auf Englisch schreiben:

____

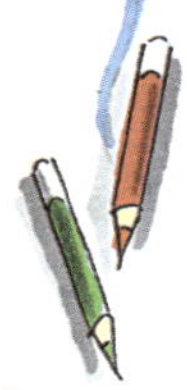

____

____

That was 

Portfolio: At School

Ich kann schon auf Englisch verstehen:

- wenn jemand von Dingen in meinem Schulranzen spricht
- wenn jemand von Dingen im Klassenzimmer spricht
- wenn jemand sagt, was er in der Schule tut
- wenn mir jemand sagt, was ich tun soll und was nicht

Ich kann schon auf Englisch sagen:

- wie die Dinge in meinem Schulranzen heißen
- wie die Dinge in meinem Klassenzimmer heißen
- wo die Gegenstände im Klassenzimmer sind
- was wir in der Schule tun
- was jemand tun soll oder nicht

Ich kann schon auf Englisch fragen:

- wo die Gegenstände im Klassenzimmer sind
- ob ich auf die Toilette gehen darf
- was jemand in seinem Schulranzen hat

Ich kann schon auf Englisch lesen:

- die Gegenstände in meinem Schulranzen
- die Gegenstände in meinem Klassenzimmer
- unsere Schulregeln

Ich kann schon auf Englisch schreiben:

- die Namen der Gegenstände in meinem Schulranzen
- die Namen der Gegenstände in meinem Klassenzimmer
- unsere Schulregeln

Ich bin mit mir sehr zufrieden.

Ich finde, es war schon ganz gut.

Ich hoffe, das wird noch besser.

Animals at the Zoo

1. Look at the animals. Write the names in the boxes.

2. Wich animals do you like? Which animals don't you like? Why?

I like ____________________, because ______________________________________

I like ____________________, ____

I don't like ____________________, because _________________________________

I don't like ____________________, ____

My favourite animal is a ____

... they are ...
funny dangerous scary beautiful cuddly big small long friendly ...

Animals at the Zoo – We're Going to the Zoo

1. Please write the correct letters in the circles. There will be two circles left.

A

See the elephants with the long trunk swinging.
Great big ears and the long trunk swinging.
Snuffing up peanuts with the long trunk swinging.
And we can stay all day!

B

See all the monkeys they're scritch-scritch scratching.
Jumping all around and scritch-scritch scratching.
Hanging by their long tails scritch-scritch scratching.
And we can stay all day!

C

There's a big black bear he's huff-puff-a-puffin'.
His coat's too heavy he's huff-puff-a-puffin'.
Don't get near that huff-puff-a-puffin'.
Or you won't stay all day!

D

Well the seals in the pool all honk-honk-honking.
Catching little fish and honk-honk-honking.
Little tiny seals all honk-honk-honking.
And we can stay all day!

2. Please tick ☑ the correct answers:

What have the elephants got?	☐ big legs	☐ a long trunk
What are the monkeys doing?	☐ They are jumping.	☐ They are eating.
What does the bear look like?	☐ white and wet	☐ big and black
What are the seals eating?	☐ fruit	☐ fish

3. Please tick ☑ the correct answers:

Who is taking us to the zoo?	☐ dog	☐ Daddy
What do you feel like after the day at the zoo?	☐ sleepy	☐ sad

Pets

1. In this puzzle there are the names of 12 pets. Can you find them all? Write them down.

					g					
				k	u	l				
			s	f	i	s	h			
		w	o	z	n	r	t	z		
	m	o	u	s	e	p	i	t	h	
d	r	w	n	r	a	t	m	o	k	r
o	c	i	n	c	p	s	t	r	p	a
g	a	a	s	d	i	p	g	t	m	b
n	t	b	u	d	g	i	e	o	b	b
d	t	e	j	k	l	d	m	i	v	i
p	a	r	r	o	t	e	p	s	z	t
d	f	t	r	w	n	r	z	e	m	p
p	i	o	b	h	a	m	s	t	e	r

2. Which pet is it? Please tick ☑ the right box.

a) It is a small pet. It has got fur. It lives in houses, but the people do not know it. It is grey. It has got a pink tail.

It is ☐ a rat ☐ a hamster .

b) It is a small pet. Many children love it. It has got fur. It has got long ears.

It is ☐ a dog ☐ a rabbit.

c) It is a pet that is sometimes small and sometimes big. It has not got fur. It has got its own house.

It is ☐ a spider ☐ a tortoise .

d) It is sometimes small and sometimes big. Most children like this pet. But it is a lot of work. It has got fur. And it has got a tail. It can be many colours.

It is ☐ a dog ☐ a budgie .

Pets – The New Pet

1. Can you read the text?

The New Pet

Anna and Michael want a new pet. They think it is a lot of fun. Mum and Dad say: "It is a lot of work. And you must pay with your own money." They go to the pet shop. "I want a dog," Anna says. "Is it a lot of work?" "Yes," the pet shop owner says. "You must feed it, give it enough water, take it for walks every day, play with it and you must brush its fur." "That is no work. It is fun," Anna says. "How much is a dog?" "200 pounds." "I have only got 10 pounds. Which pet do I get for it?" "You can get a hamster. But you need money for the cage, the straw and the food, too." Anna goes home. She is sad. But Michael has got some money, too. So they can buy the hamster tomorrow.

2. Can you answer the questions?

Which pet does Anna want first? ______________________________

Is a dog a lot of work? ______________________

What do you have to do with it? ____________________________________

____

How much is the dog? __________________

Which pet can she buy? __________________

3. Please tick ☑ the right answers.

Anna and Michael want a pet. Why?

☐ Because they want a little zoo at home. ☐ Because it is fun.

Mum and Dad do not want a pet. Why not?

☐ Because they don't like pets. ☐ Because pets are a lot of work.

Anna and Michael do not buy a pet. Why not?

☐ Because they don't like the pets there.

☐ Because they don't have enough money.

Pets – What Does a Pet Need?

1. What does a pet need?

A dog needs ______________________________

A cat needs ______________________________

A budgie needs ______________________________

2. Pets are a lot of work. Tick ✓ what you've got to do for these pets.

You've got to take it for walks every day.

You've got to play with it many times a day.

You've got to feed and water it every day.

You've got to talk to it many times a day.

You've got to clean the cage/the terrarium/the basket every week.

Pets – Which Pet Do You Want?

1. What do you tell your parents if you like a pet?

   Please fill in the missing sentences:

   Mummy, Daddy, I want a pet.

   ____

   No, I will clean it every day.

   ____

   No, it is no work for you, I will do it all.

   ____

   I have got a lot of time.

   ____

   I want a dog!
   You will get a toy dog!

   ____

2. Which pet do you want? Why?

   I want ____________________, because ______________________________

   ____

... you can do many things with it ... it is sweet and cuddly
... I can talk to it about everything ... I love scary animals

3. Which pet do you not want? Why not?

   I don't want ____________________, because ______________________________

   ____

... it is too much work ... I don't like it ... I don't have enough money
... I cannot talk to it ... I don't like scary animals

Portfolio: Animals

I can name a lot of animals.

I can write down the names of five pets and five wild animals:

____

____

I can tell which animals I like or don't like and why.

I like ____________________ , because ____________________

I like ____________________ , because ____________________

I know what a pet needs.

A ____________________ needs ____________________

Diese Wörter und Sätze über Tiere kann ich schon auf Englisch schreiben:

____

____

____

That was

Portfolio: Animals

Ich kann schon auf Englisch verstehen:

- wenn jemand von Tieren erzählt
- wenn jemand sagt, was man für die Tiere braucht
- wenn jemand sagt, was man mit den Haustieren tun muss
- wenn jemand eine Geschichte von Tieren erzählt
- wenn jemand sagt, welches Tier er mag und warum

Ich kann schon auf Englisch sagen:

- wie die Haustiere und die Zootiere heißen
- welche Tiere ich mag und warum
- welche Tiere ich nicht mag und warum nicht
- was ich für ein Haustier alles brauche
- wie ein bestimmtes Tier ist

Ich kann schon auf Englisch fragen:

- wie die Namen der Tiere sind
- ob jemand ein Tier mag

Ich kann schon auf Englisch lesen:

- die Tiernamen
- wenn jemand schreibt, ob er ein Tier mag oder nicht
- wenn jemand schreibt, warum er ein Tier mag oder nicht

Ich kann schon auf Englisch schreiben:

- die Namen der Tiere
- einige Sätze über Tiere

Ich bin mit mir sehr zufrieden.

Ich finde, es war schon ganz gut.

Ich hoffe, das wird noch besser.

Clothes – In the Wardrobe

1. In the wardrobe there are many clothes. Can you write down the names?

1 ____	2 ____	3 ____
4 ____	5 ____	6 ____
7 ____	8 ____	9 ____
10 ____	11 ____	12 a pair of ____
13 a pair of ____	14 a pair of ____	15 a pair of ____
16 a pair ____	17 a pair ____	18 a pair ____
19 a ____	20 ____	21 ____

Clothes – Put on/Take off

Put on/Take Off

1. Tell Anna which clothes she shall put on.
   You do not need all of them. Tick ✓ the clothes first.

   What shall I put on?

   Put on a ______________________

   Put on ______________________

   Put on ______________________

   ____

   ____

2. Tell Michael which clothes he shall take off.
   You do not need all of them.
   Tick ✓ the clothes first.

   What shall I take off?

   Take off the ______________________

   Take off ______________________

   Take off ______________________

   ____

   ____

The Right Clothes for Every Weather

Anna and Michael get up in the morning. They want to know what the weather is like and look out of the window. Help them to choose the right clothes:

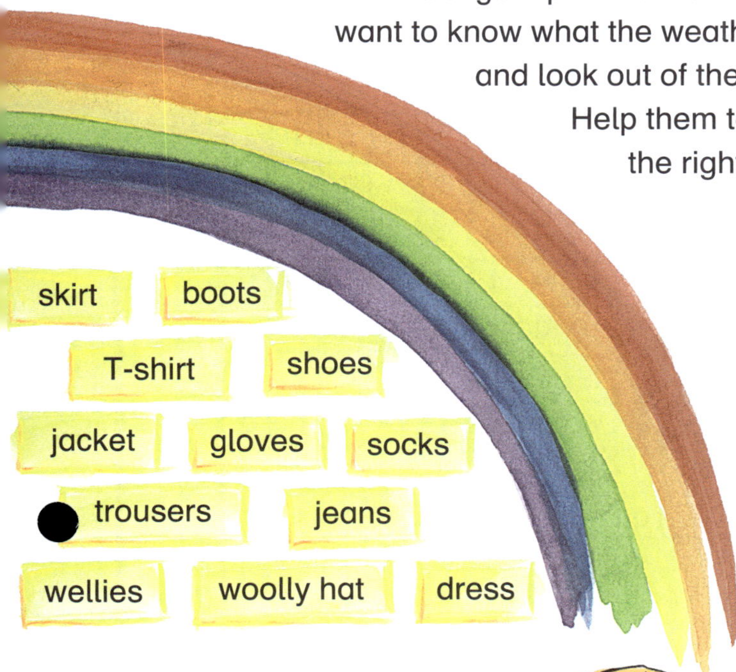

skirt | boots | T-shirt | shoes | jacket | gloves | socks | trousers | jeans | wellies | woolly hat | dress

What's the weather like? What can I wear?

When it is sunny I can wear ______________________________

____

When it is rainy I can wear ______________________________

____

When it is snowy I can wear ______________________________

____

When it is cloudy I can wear ______________________________

____

Weather – Find the Weather Words

1. Can you find the 13 words?

q	w	e	b	r	t	z	u	s	n	o	w	i	n	g	i	t	o	p	h	a	i	l
a	s	d	l	f	g	h	j	w	k	l	y	x	c	v	b	h	o	t	n	m	q	w
e	r	l	i	g	h	t	n	i	n	g	t	z	u	i	o	u	p	a	s	d	f	g
h	j	k	z	l	y	x	c	n	v	b	n	m	q	w	e	n	t	z	u	i	o	p
a	s	d	z	f	g	h	j	d	k	l	y	c	l	o	u	d	y	x	s	c	v	b
n	m	m	a	n	b	v	c	y	x	y	l	o	k	j	h	e	g	f	u	d	s	a
s	t	o	r	m	y	p	o	l	u	z	t	l	r	e	w	r	a	i	n	i	n	g
q	m	n	d	b	v	x	c	y	l	k	j	d	h	g	f	d	s	a	n	p	o	i
i	u	z	t	r	e	r	a	i	n	b	o	w	w	q	m	n	b	v	y	c	x	r

2. Write the words under the matching weather.

It is raining.

There is thunder

and lightning.

Weather – The Weather Report

1. Fill in the missing words and try to read the text.

Weather Report:
This is children's radio with the weather forecast for today.

In the morning it will be nice and  ______________ . Later, at lunchtime we expect it to be very  __________________ and eventually it will be  ________ . In the afternoon it will be  __________ and  ________ all over the country. Tomorrow it will be very  ___________ . In the evening it will be  ________ and you can watch some  ____________ . At night there will be  _____________ ______________________ and it will be very  ______________ .

2. Can you answer these questions?

What will the weather be like in the morning? ______________________

When will it be cloudy and rainy? ______________________

What can we watch? ______________________

Where will it be snowy and cold in the afternoon? ______________________

What's the Weather Like?

1. What's the weather like? Draw the weather symbol in the boxes.

There are many lovely flowers. The sky is blue.

I can wear a T-shirt and shorts. It is ____________________

It is very wet outside. I've got to wear a hat and a jacket and

special shoes. I've got to take my umbrella. ____________________

I want to stay in the house. It is very loud. Sometimes I can see something flashing like a camera outside.

______________________________ and ____________________

I don't like it outside. There are ice-balls falling from the sky.

It hurts on my head. ______________________________

Everybody loves it. First it was sunny. At the same time it started

raining. It has many lovely colours. ____________________

It is sunny. It is cloudy. It is rainy. It is snowy.
It is hot. There is a rainbow. There is hail. It is stormy. It is cold.
There is thunder and lightning. There is a blizzard. It is windy.

2. What's the weather like today?

____

Portfolio: Weather and Clothes

I can name clothes.

I can write down the names of five pieces of clothing:

____

____

I can name clothes with "a pair of".

I can write down the names of three "pairs":

A pair of ______________________ , ______________________

____

I know many kinds of weather.

I can write down what the weather is like.

It is ____

____

There is ____

____

That was 

Portfolio: Weather and Clothes

Ich kann schon auf Englisch verstehen:

- wenn jemand über Kleidung spricht
- wenn jemand sagt, was er an- oder auszieht
- wenn jemand sagt, was ich an- oder ausziehen soll
- wenn jemand vom Wetter erzählt
- wenn jemand sagt, wie das Wetter wird
- was ich bei welchem Wetter anziehen soll
- die Geschichten, die erzählt oder vorgelesen wurden

Ich kann schon auf Englisch sagen:

- wie die Kleidungsstücke heißen
- was ich an- oder ausziehe
- was jemand an- oder ausziehen soll
- wie das Wetter ist
- was jemand bei einem bestimmten Wetter anzieht

Ich kann schon auf Englisch fragen:

- wie das Wetter ist
- was ich an- oder ausziehen soll

Ich kann schon auf Englisch lesen:

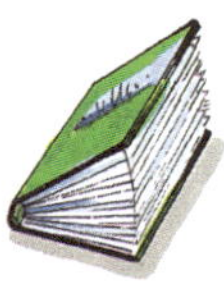

- die Namen der Kleidungsstücke
- was ich an- oder ausziehen soll
- was jemand anhat
- wie das Wetter ist

Ich kann schon auf Englisch schreiben:

- die Namen der Kleidungsstücke
- wie das Wetter ist

Ich bin mit mir sehr zufrieden.

Ich finde, es war schon ganz gut.

Ich hoffe, das wird noch besser.

Animals on a Farm – The Animals

1. Here are the names of 10 animals on a farm. Can you find them all?

w	e	c	o	w	h	g	o	a	t
r	t	z	u	i	o	o	p	l	k
g	o	o	s	e	r	g	h	h	j
f	d	c	s	a	s	h	e	e	p
y	d	o	n	k	e	y	c	n	i
v	b	c	a	t	n	w	e	r	g
t	z	k	u	i	l	k	j	h	g

2. Write down the names of the animals.

3. Guess the animal:

It is a big animal. It has fur. You can milk it.

It is a ______________________

The animal is not big. It has feathers. It has a red comb on his head.

It is a ______________________

It is a nice animal. It has soft fur. It has whiskers and likes mice.

It is a ______________________

Animals on a Farm

1. Which animals can you find? Write down the names:

Animals on a Farm – The Farm

1. Connect the pictures and the matching words.

field

meadow

stable

tractor

barn

wheelbarrow

tree

2. Look at the farm picture (page 38) again. Please fill in the missing words.

Use “next to”, “on”, “under”, “in”, “in front of” and “behind”:

The cow is ________________ the stable.

The ducks are ________________ the pond.

The cock is ________________ the henhouse.

The goat is ________________ the sheep.

The donkey is ________________ the house.

One hen is ________________ the henhouse.

The cat is ________________ the sty.

The dog is ________________ the house.

Animals on a Farm – Working on a Farm

The farmer is very busy:

He must collect eggs.

He must give water to the animals.

He must sow cereals and vegetables.

He must pick apples and pears.

He must milk the cows.

He must feed the animals.

He must clean the stables.

1. What is the farmer doing in the pictures?

He is picking the apples.

He is ______________________________

He is ______________________________

He is ______________________________

He is ______________________________

He is ______________________________

He is ______________________________

Portfolio: Animals on a Farm

I know the animals on a farm.
I can write down the names of five farm animals.

I know some things on a farm.
I can write down three things.

I know what a farmer must do.
I can write down three things what a farmer must do.

That was

Portfolio: Animals on a Farm

Ich kann schon auf Englisch verstehen:

- wenn jemand über Bauernhoftiere spricht
- wenn jemand sagt, was er auf dem Bauernhof tut
- wenn jemand sagt, was es auf dem Bauernhof gibt
- wenn jemand erzählt, was ein Bauer tut
- wenn jemand sagt, wo die Dinge auf dem Bild sind

Ich kann schon auf Englisch sagen:

- wie die Bauernhoftiere heißen
- wo etwas auf einem Bauernhof ist
- was ein Bauer tut
- was jemand auf dem Bauernhof tun soll

Ich kann schon auf Englisch fragen:

- wo etwas auf dem Bauernhof ist
- wie die Tiere heißen
- was der Bauer tut

Ich kann schon auf Englisch lesen:

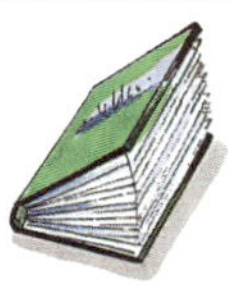

- die Namen der Tiere
- die Namen der Gegenstände auf dem Bauernhofbild
- was der Bauer tut
- wo etwas auf dem Bild ist

Ich kann schon auf Englisch schreiben:

- die Namen der Bauernhoftiere
- die Namen der Gegenstände auf dem Bauernhofbild

Ich bin mit mir sehr zufrieden.

Ich finde, es war schon ganz gut.

Ich hoffe, das wird noch besser.

My Body

1. Write the correct names in the boxes.

nose neck foot head leg ear mouth
body hair eye arm face hand

2. How many of them have you got?

I've got ________________ legs. I've got ________________ feet.

I've got ________________ arms. I've got ________________ head.

I've got ________________ fingers. ______________________________

______________________________ ______________________________

______________________________ ______________________________

______________________________ ______________________________

My Body – The Parts of the Body

1. Can you find these parts of the body, too? Connect the pictures and the matching words.

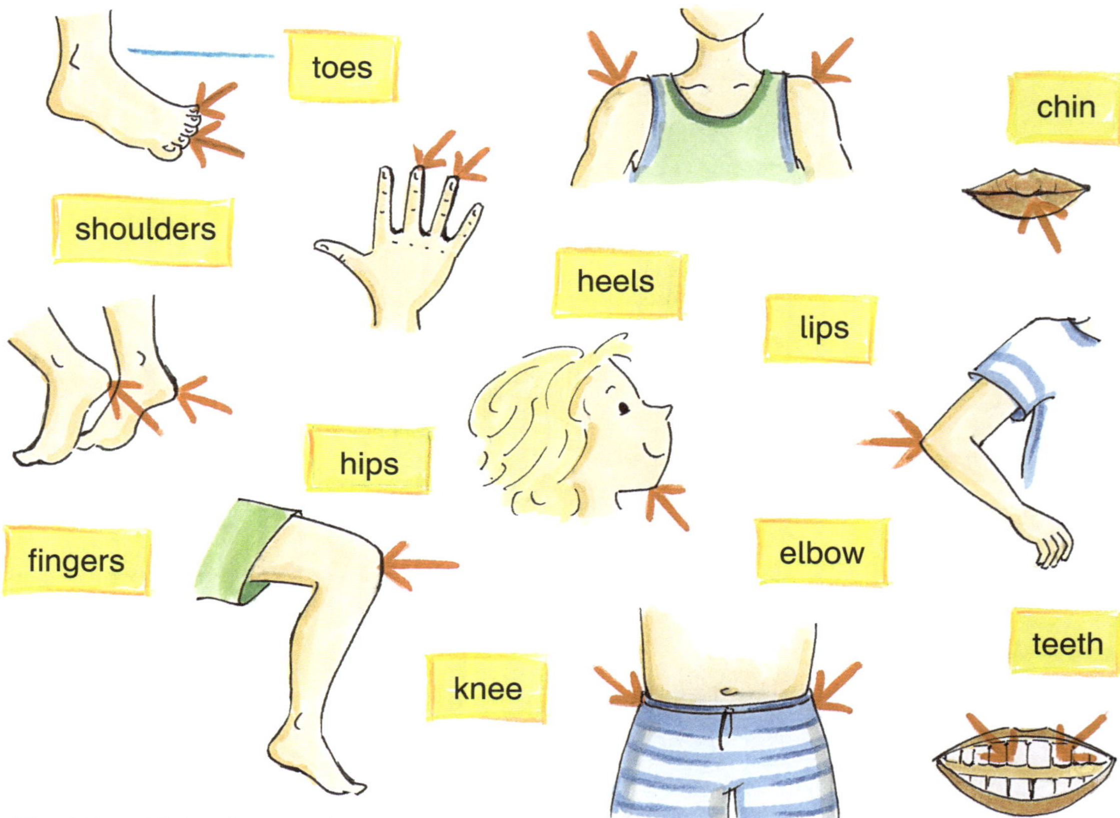

2. Find the 15 body words.

s	x	n	e	c	k	h	t	x	h
h	e	y	e	s	f	e	e	t	a
o	f	c	b	k	n	e	e	o	i
u	a	h	o	m	e	l	t	e	r
l	c	i	d	o	a	s	h	s	x
d	e	n	y	u	n	l	i	p	s
e	a	r	s	t	s	e	b	r	m
r	n	l	x	h	o	g	l	t	n

3. Cross out the wrong words.

Michael gets up.

Michael sits on his bed. His feet / eyes are on the floor. His arms / eyes are not open yet.

He stretches his nose / arms and stands up. He washes his face / knees and brushes his mouth / hair.

My Body – What We Can Do With Our Body

1. Can you understand the text? Circle all words concerning the body.

Simon says

Anna goes to school. She puts her schoolbag on her shoulders. At school she raises her hand when she wants to say something. The teacher plays a little game with them: Simon says … She says: „Simon says: stand up! Simon says: clap your hands! Simon says: stomp your feet! Touch your nose!“ Anna touches her nose. All children laugh. The teacher did not say: „Simon says…“
In the end all children sit on their chairs.

2. Can you read this?

Clap your hands three times.

Snap your fingers five times.

Touch your nose with your right fingers.

Touch your left knee with your left hand.

Put your right hand on your mouth.

Lift up your left foot.

Touch both eyes with both hands.

Touch both shoulders with both hands.

Touch your toes without bending your knees.

Put your right foot on your chair.

3. Finish the sentences.

I can touch with my ____________________

I can smell with my ____________________

I can see with my ____________________

I can hear with my ____________________

I can speak with my ____________________

I can walk with my ____________________

mouth nose hands
legs eyes arms teeth
heels ears body

You do not need all the words.

I did not need:

____________ ____________

____________ ____________

My Body – Here We Go Round the Mulberry Bush

In the Bathroom

There are many things you do in the bathroom and many things you need in a bathroom.

1. Can you write the correct words under the matching pictures?

__________ __________ __________ __________

__________ __________ __________ __________

face-cloth have a bath wash hands have a shower
wash face brush teeth comb hair brush hair towel toothbrush
toothpaste wash hair shampoo soap hairbrush comb

__________ __________ __________ __________

 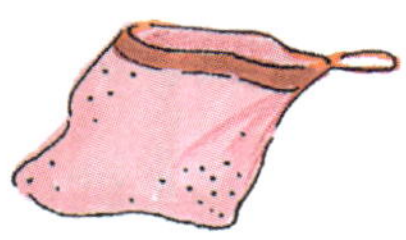 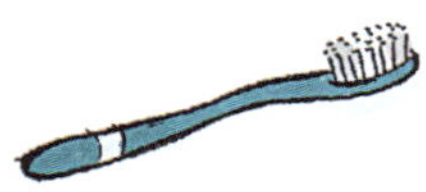 

__________ __________ __________ __________

2. What do you need? 

I wash my  __________ with a 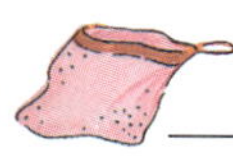 __________.

I brush my  __________ with a 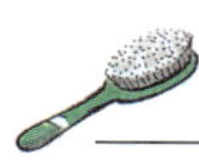 __________ and a 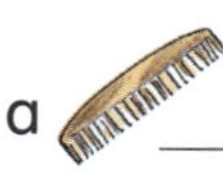 __________.

 __________ with a 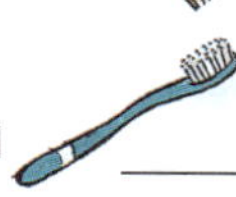 __________

and  __________.

Portfolio: My Body

I know the parts of my body.
I can write down the names of five parts of my body.

____

____

I can write down how I move my body.
Please write down three things.

I can jump, ________________________________

I know what I can do with the parts of my body.
Write down three things.

I can smell with my nose, __________________________

____

That was 

Portfolio: My Body

Ich kann schon auf Englisch verstehen:

- wenn jemand über Körperteile spricht
- wenn jemand sagt, wie ich mich bewegen soll
- wenn jemand sagt, was ich mit den Körperteilen mache
- wenn jemand erzählt, was er mit seinem Körper tut

Ich kann schon auf Englisch sagen:

- wie die Körperteile heißen
- was ich mit meinen Körperteilen tue
- was jemand mit seinem Körper tun soll

Ich kann schon auf Englisch fragen:

- wie die Körperteile heißen
- was ich mit meinem Körper tun soll

Ich kann schon auf Englisch lesen:

- die Namen der Körperteile
- was ich mit meinem Körper tun soll
- was jemand mit seinem Körper tut
- was ich mit welchem Teil des Körpers mache

Ich kann schon auf Englisch schreiben:

- die Namen der Körperteile
- was ich mit welchem Teil des Körpers mache

Ich bin mit mir sehr zufrieden.

Ich finde, es war schon ganz gut.

Ich hoffe, das wird noch besser.

Food – Salad and Soup

1. Here you can see a salad bowl and a soup bowl. Can you name the fruit for a fruit salad and the vegetables for a soup?

2. If you read the letters in the boxes, you find another fruit and another vegetable.

1	2	3	4	5	6

1	2	3	4	5	6

Food – At the Market

1. Please read the text.

Anna and Michael at the Market

Anna and Michael go shopping at the market. “Good morning,” the woman says. “Good morning,” Anna and Michael answer. “Can I help you?” Anna and Michael think. What did Mum say? They shall buy pears and onions. “I’d like five pears and two onions, please,” Michael says. “Here you are,” the woman says. Anna says: “Thank you.” “You’re welcome. Good bye,” the woman says. The pears look really nice. Michael takes one and eats it. “Michael!” Anna shouts. “We’ve got to buy 5 pears.” But Michael enjoys his pear. “Good bye!” he says to the woman.

2. Let’s go shopping at the market. Put the sentences in the correct order:

1 ______________________________

2 ______________________________

3 ______________________________

4 ______________________________

____

5 ______________________________

6 ______________________________

7 ______________________________

8 ______________________________

Can I help you?

Thank you.

You’re welcome. Good bye.

I’d like five pears and two onions, please.

Good bye.

Here you are.

Good morning.

Good morning.

Food – Let´s Get a Drink

1. There are some drinks. Can you name them?

______________________ ______________________

______________________ ______________________

______________________ ______________________

coffee tea hot chocolate milk lemonade orange juice

2. You need something to fill the drinks in. What can you fill in...

... a cup? A cup of coffee,

a cup of ______________________ , a cup of ______________________

... a mug? A mug of coffee,

a mug of ______________________ , a mug of ______________________

... a glass? A glass of milk,

a glass of ______________________ , a glass of ______________________

... a bottle? A bottle of orange juice,

a bottle of ______________________ , a bottle of ______________________

... a carton? A carton of milk,

a carton of ______________________ , a carton of ______________________

3. At the Restaurant

Can you write a dialogue? Order a glass of lemonade, please.

You: ______________

Water: ______________

Y: ______________________________

W: ______________________________

Y: ______________________________

W: ______________________________

Food – The Meals

1. What meal do we have?

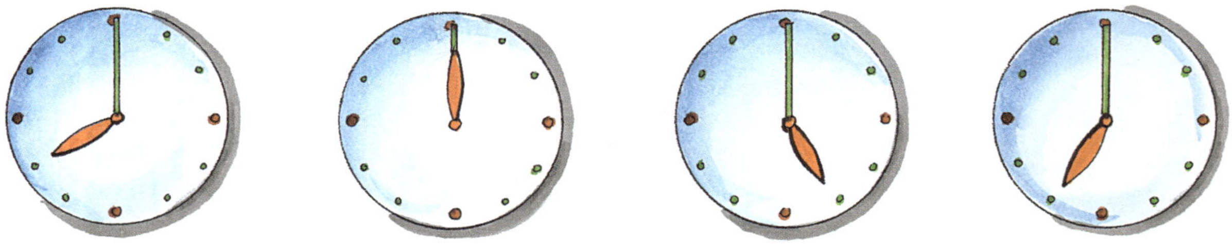

dinner   breakfast   lunch   tea

2. What do you like for breakfast? Write the words and connect them to the pictures.

bread   butter   jam   honey   cheese   ham   cornflakes   cereal
milk   sugar   egg   British breakfast   sandwich   cake   biscuits

3. This is my favourite breakfast:

For breakfast I like ______________________________

Food – Let's Lay the Table

Let's Lay the Table

1. Here are the descriptions of dishes, cutlery and other items you need to lay a table. Can you find these things in the picture?

1 It is round. You eat from it. It is a **plate**.
2 It has got a handle. It is small. There is coffee or tea in it. It is a **cup**.
3 It is under a cup. It is round. It is a **saucer**.
4 It lies on the table. When it is dirty you must wash it. It is a **table cloth**.
5 It is a big cup. It is a **mug**.
6 It is big. It stands in the middle of the table. There is soup in it. It is a **soup bowl**.
7 It is big. It is in the middle of the table, too. There is tea in it. It is a **teapot**.
8 You can see through it. You put lemonade or juice in it. It is a **glass**.
9 It looks like the big one in the middle of the table. It is for a dessert.
It is a **dessert bowl**.
10 It is something to stick in meat or pizza. It is a **fork**.
11 It is something to cut food. It is a **knife**.
12 You eat soup with it. It is a **spoon**.
13 You've got it to wipe your mouth when you've finished eating. It is a **napkin**.
14 You put sugar in it. It is a **sugar dish**.
15 You put milk for the tea in it. It is a **milk jug**.
16 You cook food in it. It is a **pot**.

Food – What Do You Like for Dinner?

1. What do you like for dinner? Write the words and connect them to the pictures.

______________________ ______________________
______________________ ______________________
______________________ ______________________
______________________ ______________________
______________________ ______________________
____

pasta pizza salad chips hamburger fish meat
sausages beans soup vegetables

2. This is my favourite dinner: For dinner I like ______________________ .

3. Can you read the text? Fill in the missing words.

5 o'Clock Tea

This is a scone → 

In  ____________ people have  ________ at  ____________ .
They stop working and drink  ________ or  __________ or
 ______________ and eat  ____________ ,  __________ ,
 ____________ ,  ___________ or  ____________ .
A scone is a typical British cake. There is  __________ and  __________
on it and it tastes very sweet. People in Britain like to drink strong black tea with
 ________ .

coffee tea cake biscuits hot chocolate milk scones
jam cream sandwiches Britain 5 o'clock tea cookies

Portfolio: Food

I know some drinks.
I can write down the names of three drinks.

____

I know some things for breakfast.
I can write down three things.

____

I know many things to eat.
I can write down five things.

____

____

That was 

Portfolio: Food

Ich kann schon auf Englisch verstehen:

- wenn jemand über Essen spricht
- wenn jemand etwas zu essen bestellt
- wenn jemand fragt, was ich essen möchte
- wenn jemand von den Mahlzeiten erzählt
- wenn jemand erzählt, was er gerne isst

Ich kann schon auf Englisch sagen:

- wie die Dinge zu essen und zu trinken heißen
- dass ich etwas zu trinken bestellen möchte
- was ich essen oder trinken möchte
- was ich gerne esse
- wie die Mahlzeiten auf Englisch heißen

Ich kann schon auf Englisch fragen:

- was jemand gerne isst

Ich kann schon auf Englisch lesen:

- die Namen der verschiedenen Mahlzeiten
- die Namen der Getränke und ihrer Gefäße
- die Namen der Speisen
- ein Gespräch im Restaurant
- einen Ausschnitt aus der Geschichte

Ich kann schon auf Englisch schreiben:

- die Namen der verschiedenen Mahlzeiten
- die Namen der Getränke und ihrer Gefäße

Ich bin mit mir sehr zufrieden.

Ich finde, es war schon ganz gut.

Ich hoffe, das wird noch besser.

Toys – Where Is Bobby?

1. Please read the text.

Where Is Bobby?

Can you find the names for toys?

Cross out the wrong words.

Anna tidies up her room. She puts her [gameboy / cat] onto the bookshelf.

The [teddybears / apples] and the [schoolbags / dolls] are on the bookshelf, too.

The boxes with the [building sets / sandwiches], the [T-shirts / jigsaw puzzles] and the [games / socks] are in the cupboard.

Michael's room is a big mess. He must tidy up, too.

Bobby the dog watches him.

Michael scoops his clothes, his [toy cars / chocolate], his [chewing gum / scocter], his [ball / ice cream], his [jigsaw puzzles / bananas], his [ears / games] and his [building sets / feet] into his wardrobe.

Mum comes in and sees the tidy room. She is happy. But then...

They hear a "woof" coming out of the wardrobe.

Toys – There Are Many Toys

1. There are many toys in the children's bedroom.
   Which toys can you find? How many?

There are two dolls, ____

____

____

____

2. Which toys do you like? Why?

I like the ______________________________ ,

because ____

it is fun, many children can play with them, it is interesting, you can learn a lot, you can use it outside, you can cuddle it, I can build houses with them, I can play many different games with it (them), I can play with my parents…

3. Which toys do you not like? Why not?

I do not like the ______________________________ ,

because ____

it is boring, it is only for boys/girls, it is for little children, I cannot use it in the house, I am too old for it, I cannot play with other children, I cannot use it outside…

Toys – In the Playground

1. In the playground you can see a lot of things.

swing   watering can   see-saw   slide   bicycle   sandbox   bucket
shovel   bench   wheelbarrow   tree   bush   path   fence   merry-go-round

2. Can you name the things?

1 ____________	2 ____________	3 ____________
4 ____________	5 ____________	6 ____________
7 ____________	8 ____________	9 ____________
10 ____________	11 ____________	12 ____________
13 ____________	14 ____________	15 ____________

3. Where are the things?

The shovel is ____________ the sandbox.

The bicycle is ____________ the bench.

The bush is ____________ the slide.

The watering can is ____________ the sandbox.

The mum is sitting ____________ the bench.

Toys – What Can You Do with Your Friends?

1. My best friends are ______________________________

____

2. What do you like doing with your friends?
Connect the pictures with the matching words.

reading

playing basketball

watching TV

playing instruments

singing/listening to music

riding bikes

dancing

playing football

riding horses

swimming

going shopping

playing games

playing computer games

going to the playground

3. What do you like doing with your friends?

My friends and I like ______________________________

We ______________________________

Portfolio: Toys and Leisure

I know some toys.
I can write down the names of five things.

____

____

I know some things in a playground.
I can write down five things.

____

____

I can tell what I like doing with my friends.

I like ____

____

____

That was 

Portfolio: Toys and Leisure

Ich kann schon auf Englisch sagen:

- wie die Spielsachen heißen
- womit ich gerne spiele
- was ich mit meinen Freunden gerne spiele
- warum ich ein Spielzeug mag oder nicht mag

Ich kann schon auf Englisch fragen:

- womit jemand gerne spielt und warum

Ich kann schon auf Englisch lesen:

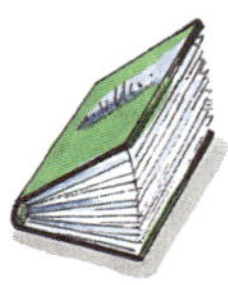

- die Namen der Spielsachen und Spielgeräte
- womit jemand gerne spielt
- was jemand gerne mit seinen Freunden unternimmt

Ich kann schon auf Englisch schreiben:

- die Namen der verschiedenen Spielsachen
- die Namen der Spielgeräte auf dem Spielplatz
- was ich mit Freunden unternehme

Ich bin mit mir sehr zufrieden.

Ich finde, es war schon ganz gut.

Ich hoffe, das wird noch besser.

Let´s Spell - The English Alphabet

This is the English Alphabet. Can you read it?

A - ei	B - biː	C - siː	D - diː	E - iː	F - ef	G - dʒiː
H - eitʃ	I - ai	J - dʒei	K - kei	L - el	M - em	N - en
O - ou	P - piː	Q - kjuː	R - aːr	S - es	T - tiː	U - juː
V - viː	W - double juː		X - eks	Y - wai	Z - zed	

This is the Alphabet Song:

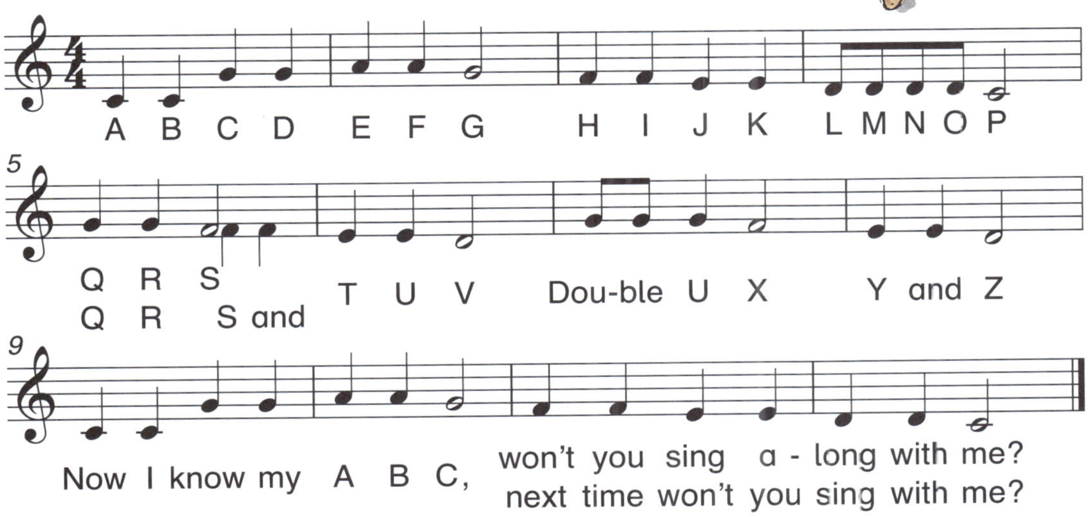

Please work with your partner. Think about words.
Say the letters and your partner writes down the words:

Can You Remember - Quiz

Can You Remember?

1. Please introduce yourself:

   What's your name? ______________________

   How old are you? ______________________

   Where do you live? ______________________

2. At School: Can you name five things in your schoolbag?

   ____

3. In the classroom: Can you name three things in the classroom?

   ____

4. Big numbers: Can you write the words for these numbers?

   24: ______________ 72: ______________ 39: ______________

5. Colours: Can you write the correct names of these colours?

 ______________  ______________  ______________

6. Animals: Can you read the texts and write the names of these animals?

   It lives in a zoo. It is dangerous. It lives in water. It is brown and green.

   ____

   It is small. It has got eight legs. Many people don't like it.

   ____

7. Clothes: Which clothes do you put on in winter?

   ____

8. Food and drink: What is your favourite breakfast?

   ____

9. Toys: What do you like playing with your friends?

   ____

Well done! You're a genius! See you next year!